THE REFORMATION
IN ENGLAND

by
Raymond Edwards

*All booklets are published thanks to the
generous support of the members of the
Catholic Truth Society*

CATHOLIC TRUTH SOCIETY
PUBLISHERS TO THE HOLY SEE

Contents

Introduction

The Accepted Version

English-speaking Catholics are at a disadvantage when considering the history of their faith. For generations, and throughout the English-speaking world, the accepted accounts of the great religious upheavals of the sixteenth and seventeenth centuries, which led to the division of historic Western Christendom into Catholic and Protestant camps, were almost all written by non-Catholics, who saw these religious changes as an inevitable and wholesome part of the growth and development of the modern democratic state.

The story went broadly like this: at the start of the fifteenth century, a movement of religious reform began in Germany against the venality and superstition endemic in the medieval Catholic Church. Based on a renewed study of the Bible, and a simple piety, this reform freed Christianity from the encrusted and politicized grasp of an autocratic Papacy, and society in general from the repressive hands of the Church. This allowed science, commerce, and representative democratic institutions to flourish, and thus brought about the benefits of modern Western civilization[1]. This development is best seen in

England, where the excesses of the more extreme reforming movements of continental Europe, and the corresponding reaction by Catholic monarchs, were both avoided; thus we have the glories of the Elizabethan age, and the great upward trend of English political and commercial institutions throughout the following centuries (only briefly impeded by the fortunately unsuccessful efforts of some deluded Englishmen, abetted by foreign powers, to re-impose Catholicism on an unwilling people).

Even now, when few if any historians would endorse this "Whig" model of history in general terms, somehow an exception seems to be made for religious history. In historiography, anti-Catholic feeling still runs deep, if unconscious. Even some Catholics are vaguely troubled by a sense that the reformation was a necessary evil, that the late medieval Church, in England as elsewhere, was hopelessly corrupt, that the tide of history was (and is) against them. There are still a few historians who would support an only slightly modified view of this traditional picture; but the consensus amongst scholars is decidedly against them. So what actually did happen? How, and when, and why did England stop being a Catholic country?

In the account that follows, I focus on events in England, for a number of reasons. The majority of my readers are likely to be most familiar with this story, or some version of it; the course of events in Scotland, at this time an independent country, is quite distinct, although the stories do at times intersect; I do not have the space to treat it here in extenso. Moreover, there is a good argument for placing the events that made England into a Protestant state at the heart of the subsequent religious history of Europe. Without the support of the English crown, it may be argued that continental Protestantism would not have survived the Catholic reaction of the late sixteenth and early seventeenth centuries. Whatever the truth of this, the English experience of Reformation is critical for the development of Christianity in the West.

The Continental Background

On All Saints Day, 1517, or so the story goes, a thirty-four year old German Augustinian friar, who taught at the University in Wittenberg, nailed onto the door of the Castle Church there a list of opinions on the subject of indulgences[2]. His name was Martin Luther. These opinions, the famous ninety-five theses, were in the form of a recognized academic exercise, proposing disputed statements for debate and refutation. They were not, as such, a declaration of war or a manifesto, more a series of debating points. Luther had privately, for some years, rejected the scholastic theology normal to his time, and in which he had been educated; instead, he based his own theological insights (it was at this stage scarcely a system) on the study of parts of the Pauline corpus, particularly the Letter to the Romans. There, Luther detected the concept of "justification by faith", whereby what is important in our being at rights with God is not any outward penance, or specific work of religion (prayer, pilgrimage, almsgiving, what have you) but a simple act of faith in God as our Redeemer. One of the consequences of this insight was an objection to the practice of indulgences, that is a guarantee by the Church that, in exchange for the performance of a specific act (whether a prayer, a pilgrimage, almsgiving, or going on Crusade) a certain proportion of the temporal punishment still owing for a (forgiven) sin, conventionally denominated in terms of "days in Purgatory", would be remitted. The specific indulgence that provoked Luther's objection was issued by the twenty-seven year old Prince Archbishop of Mainz, and could be obtained by almsgiving. The resulting monies were for a number of ends, including the defraying of debts incurred by the Archbishop in obtaining a dispensation from the Pope for holding his see in plurality with the Archbishopric of Magdeburg and the administration of the diocese of Halberstadt.[3] Ultimately, then, the alms given to obtain the indulgence would go to the Pope's coffers; the heavy expenses of rebuilding St Peter's (Michelangelo's version of Bramante's design was finally completed only in 1626) meant that the Holy See was in pressing need of cash. Nowhere in the ninety-five theses, however, is Luther's theology of justification by faith spelt out; it is no more than implicit.

Luther's attack on indulgences soon gained a wider significance. The doctrine and practice of indulgences relied on Papal authority: the Pope established the conditions under which any indulgence could be gained and, by his "power of the Keys", guaranteed its supernatural efficacy. To deny indulgences was to call the Pope mistaken. This point was made to Luther in 1518 by Cardinal Cajetan, the Pope's legate to the German Empire; Luther responded by denying Papal authority, and appealing to a General Council of the Church[4]. The following year, Luther was roundly trounced in public debate by Johann Eck, a renowned theologian, who forced him to concede that many of his opinions were identical with those of the Bohemian John Huss, who had been condemned and burnt by the 1415 Council of Constance. Luther admitted that in his view many of Huss's condemned opinions (denial of Papal authority, private interpretation of the text of Scripture, and so on) were truly Christian, and thus could not be validly condemned by anyone. As well as denying the authority of the Pope, then, Luther had now also denied that of a General Council.

Sola Scriptura

Where was certainty in religious belief to be found? Luther appealed to the simple text of the Bible - sola scriptura, the Word alone; but interpreted by whom? This is the heart of the problem of "reformed" Christianity: lacking a criterion for authoritative discernment between conflicting interpretations of scriptural texts (a criterion provided in Catholic theology by the teaching office of the magisterium guaranteed by the Pope) the believer is driven back into his own private judgement. This makes reformation Christianities naturally and inevitably fissiparous; a contested opinion cannot be resolved except by an appeal to force external to the Church.

During 1520, Luther applied his newly ungoverned interpretative skills to various scriptural texts and produced a number of practical conclusions, which approach to a system. The model of Church governance by the Pope, which perpetuated various unscriptural abuses, must be broken by the secular power - the German princes. The whole fabric of pardons, dispensations, indulgences, clerical celibacy, processions, pilgrimages, prayer for the dead, and the seven sacraments of the Church (Luther admitted only the two "scriptural" sacraments of Baptism and the Eucharist): all these things were unscriptural, and a denial of (for Luther) the central truth that we are justified by faith alone. Luther's theological programme was even now intimately linked to a political method: the unilateral or concerted action by German princes against the consensus of the Empire. In objecting to what he considered the religious tyranny of the Papacy, Luther was driven to advocate the direct government of the Church by local rulers.

In June 1520, Pope Leo X issued a Bull, Exsurge Domine, condemning Luther's opinions as heretical, and giving him two months to recant under threat of excommunication. Luther responded by burning the Bull publicly. In January 1521, his excommunication was made absolute; after an abortive attempt by the recently elected German Emperor, Charles V, to persuade Luther to compromise and retract, he was also, in May of that year, placed under the Ban of the Empire. His religious obstinacy had now become in addition a political rebellion. These exclusively religious quarrels were politically very convenient to some princes in northern Germany, who were disaffected in their relations with Charles. Germany was then a loose confederation of sovereign states and cities, small and large, some ruled by bishops, all under the nominal overlordship of the Emperor, who was elected by the more prominent German princes.

'Protestants'

In 1529, princes sympathetic to Luther at the Imperial Diet, or meeting, at Speyer, issued a "protest" against the Emperor and his Catholic allies; from this point, Luther's adherents were called "Protestants". In 1531, Protestant princes and cites, most in northern Germany, formed a political confederation, the Schmalkaldic League, in opposition to the Emperor. Thus an originally religious argument assumes a political dimension; were it not for this, Luther's dissent is unlikely to have lasted beyond his own lifetime.

Local political conditions throughout the Empire, however, favoured the success of Protestant ideas in some areas. One rich field was the quasi-independent Swiss city states, where regional particularism allied well with religious innovation. The clearest example is Geneva, where from 1536 on the governance of the city was in the hands of a theocratic council of elders dominated by John Calvin, a French lawyer and amateur theologian whose codification and logical extension of reformist principles in his Institutes of Christian Religion represent the least attractive side of Protestant theology. He argues for the necessary predestination of all people either to salvation or damnation, for the rightful rule of "the elect" (a self-selecting group who know themselves to be saved), the irreformable wickedness of Catholicism, and the redundancy of sacramental theology; for Calvin, "sacraments" were merely symbolical actions. The best recent practical analogy to his puritanical rule over Geneva is that of the Taleban in Afghanistan.

The Church in England

Insofar as anyone in England took any notice of Martin Luther and his followers, reactions were overwhelmingly hostile. A refutation of Luther's attack on the Sacraments was put together by University theologians, revised by Thomas More, and issued under the nominal authorship of the King, Henry VIII, in 1521. A grateful Pope Leo X gave him the title Fidei Defensor, which (oddly enough) appears on English coinage to this day. Some few reform-minded intellectuals evinced an enthusiasm for Luther's doctrines, and the remaining cells of Lollards, England's home-grown and generally despised heretics, took encouragement from them; but the vast mass of the populace was instinctively opposed - nor was there underlying social unrest, or a visible and lucrative system of indulgence-peddling, as had in Germany provided a field for dissent to germinate in. England was on the face of it the least likely country in Europe to turn Protestant.

Religious life in England was flourishing. There were roughly nine and a half thousand parish churches, and upwards of eight hundred religious houses (of monks, nuns, and friars, of dozens of different orders); plus countless lay institutions - craft guilds, pious associations and confraternities - devoted to charitable works and to prayer for the dead, which was also the main activity of countless small chantry chapels endowed for the purpose. There were something like forty thousand secular priests in the country, whether having the charge of a parish or making a living from endowed or freelance prayer and Masses, and another ten thousand or so in the various religious orders. There were, also, about two thousand nuns. Including the various deacons and subdeacons in training for the priesthood, this made a total number of professional religious of at least sixty thousand - one in forty of the population. Ordained priests represented perhaps one adult male in twenty-five. Nor was this religion stagnant; detailed studies of the early 1500s have shown a high level of voluntary expenditure on renewing church fabric and decoration (English woodcarving and statuary was internationally famous) and a rich devotional life centred around processions on great feast days, mystery plays, pilgrimages, intense devotion to local patron saints, and the broader social cohesion brought by fund-raising activities such as parish ales. At every level, English society was saturated with the Catholic faith.

'New learning'

In common with much of Europe, England was starting to encounter something of the "new learning". This term later became almost shorthand for "Protestant dissent in religion", but in origin it was not so. The fifteenth century had seen a growth in "humanist" learning, the close antiquarian study and imitation of the monuments of antiquity both written and made. Some spur to this was given by the large quantity of Greek manuscripts that found their way onto the western market after the Fall of Constantinople to the Turks in 1453; more by the activities of unscrupulous book-hunters, who made a business of abstracting rare works from the libraries of monasteries and other religious houses.

Printing

The spread of the new technology of the printed book made this interest in the antique potentially not just the fad of a few, but a goad to the whole literate class. By the sixteenth century, the emphasis of this movement had settled on the provision and study of accurate texts of the Bible and the Church Fathers. The more reflective and pious of these scholars (such as Erasmus in the Low Countries, or John Colet and Thomas More in England) naturally saw in patristic witness against the corruption of the Gospel an analogy to the contemporary situation of the Church. As in every age, the Church was in need of reform: bishops and clergy were often worldly, unfaithful to their vows, preoccupied with money and status, heedless of those notionally under their care. Some critics, more extreme, saw superstition and wilful misleading everywhere. None of this agitation was new, or necessarily unhelpful; there is nothing in Erasmus, say, that you cannot also find in Bernard of Clairvaux, or a host of other medieval churchmen exercised about the state of Christendom. The difference in the sixteenth century, in England as elsewhere, is in two things: first, the now commonplace appeal to the Greek or Hebrew text of Scripture (not in fact necessarily any more textually accurate than the Latin Vulgate it sought to supplant) in support of an otherwise contentious interpretation, which might give it a veneer of plausibility especially to those who Greek was shaky, or nil; second, the ability via the printing press for arguments, pamphlets, commentaries and expostulations to be circulated in very large numbers. The combination of these factors, with the existence of a growing class of literate laity, meant that what in a previous generation might have been a purely local phenomenon, like (say) the reform movement of Savonarola in Florence, could readily enter on an Europe-wide stage, clad in the borrowed finery of Greek and patristic learning, and with a range of effect limited only by the printer's capacity to circulate books.

An illuminating figure is the translator and polemicist William Tyndale. In 1522, his proposal for an English

Bible was rejected by the Bishop of London, for whom (as for most clergy) vernacular scriptures were closely associated with the anticlericalism of the Lollard movement, and more recently with Luther's dissent. Tyndale then moved to Cologne, and had his translation printed and smuggled into England. It made little impact at the time; his subsequent fame is based mainly on the wholesale borrowing of his version by much later official English Protestant translations. Tyndale also wrote several extensive works of Lutheran apologetic, which were ably rebutted by Thomas More (writing in the intervals of his many other responsibilities). Tyndale is at this period a very marginal figure.

The King's Great Cause

England in the 1520s was a country warily peaceful. The bloody and protracted civil wars of the previous century ("the Wars of the Roses") had ended in 1485 with the victory of Henry VIII's father, an obscure Welshman called Henry Tudor who had by descent only a tenuous claim to the throne (he was the great-grandson of an illegitimate son of a younger son of Edward III). He was in plain language a usurper. Henry VII, as he styled himself, married Elizabeth, the legitimist or Yorkist heiress, and devoted himself to economy at home and caution abroad. He had stood aloof from the convoluted and bloody business of European politics, even with regard to France, England's hereditary and inevitable enemy - he had threatened war, but apart from a brief and abortive siege of Boulogne in 1495, no actual fighting took place. Rather than the chivalric adventures traditionally seen as the proper business of the medieval king, indeed of warrior nobility as a whole, Henry VII concentrated on the arts of peace; or, more prosaically, on making money. To the end of consolidating his international position, he arranged the marriage of his elder son Arthur to Catherine of Aragon, younger daughter of the King of Spain. As well as aligning himself with the principal European counterbalance to France (and France's ally Scotland) the marriage brought a considerable dowry - fully 100,000 crowns in hand, plus the settlement of Catherine's large personal fortune. The marriage was solemnized in 1501 - Catherine was sixteen, Prince Arthur fifteen. After only a few months, Arthur died of a fever. In order to preserve the alliance, and retain Catherine's dowry, Henry VII (after briefly considering marrying the young widow himself) arranged her betrothal to his younger son, Henry, then only nine years old. For this, marriage to a deceased brother's wife, the King's agents secured a dispensation from the Pope, Julius II. On his father's death in 1509, the seventeen year old Henry cast off the fiscal and political restraint that had characterized his policy. He began to spend lavishly, and (casting himself in the mould of his predecessors in the Hundred Years War) opened hostilities with France. He also finally married Catherine.

England was intermittently at war with France, in alliance with the Holy Roman Empire, for most of the next two decades; the elaborate diplomatic efforts of Henry's Chancellor, Thomas Wolsey (Archbishop of York, and a Cardinal from 1515) sought to position England as a power-broker between the two great continental powers without, in the end, a great deal of success or advantage. Nevertheless this appealed to Henry's desire to cut a great figure on the international stage. It also left him very short of money - both war and diplomacy were very expensive.

Anne Boleyn

The lack of a male heir to the throne was a substantial perceived problem. The Queen had given birth to a daughter, Mary, in 1516. By 1525, after a series of miscarriages, it became clear that Catherine, now forty, could not bear any more children. By this time, her nephew, Charles, was the Emperor we have already encountered. Henry for some time had not been faithful to his wife, and had kept a series of mistresses, at least one of whom bore him an illegitimate son. At this stage, the figure of Anne Boleyn first appears. She had been one of Queen Catherine's ladies-in-waiting since 1522; her sister, Mary, had been the King's mistress for some time, but was now out of favour. When Anne first caught Henry's eye, she was in her early twenties[5]. Her father was a Norfolk gentleman much employed by Henry and his father as a diplomat; her mother was a Howard[6]. Anne had spent some time at the French court, and had acquired an informed sympathy for Lutheranism, and something of a reputation as a heartbreaker: at least two possible engagements had been broken off as unsuitable. Unlike many women in her position, she was not willing simply to enter the royal bed. She would do so only if she could be Queen. Henry had convinced himself that his failure to produce a male heir was God's judgement on his marriage to his dead brother's wife[7]. If, as he suspected, this was against the law of God, even the Pope could not dispense from it; his marriage was no marriage, his child Mary a bastard, the fruit of an incestuous union. If the Church were to recognise this, he would (he believed) be free to marry Anne Boleyn, and get a male heir[8]. For this to happen, however, would mean not only divorcing the aunt of the Holy Roman Emperor, Charles V, the most powerful man in Europe, but also convincing the Pope. As one Pope had granted the original dispensation, so must another rescind it.

This talk of divorces and dispensations may suggest for the modern reader that the sixteenth century view of marriage was not unlike that common in Western civil society today. However the situations are very different. Throughout the medieval period, and later, marriages were very frequently contracted to seal an alliance between families, perhaps with substantial implications in land, commercial activity, or (at a Royal level) diplomatic relations. Moreover they were often arranged on behalf of very young children years before they could lawfully be contracted. Under these circumstances, given the very high infant mortality rate, situations analogous to Henry VIII's were not uncommon: the son of one great family might be publicly (and bindingly) betrothed to the daughter of another; one of the children might die before they reached majority, and yet the families still wish to cement their alliance, requiring a dispensation to marry a brother or sister of the deceased. Alternatively, changing circumstances could mean the breaking off of a betrothal and marriage instead to a close connexion of the original intended. The potentially complex field of medieval and early modern marriage brokerage is much more closely analogous to contemporary business mergers and acquisitions than to today's divorce courts; the elaborate mechanism of canon law existed to regulate and harmonize potential conflicts between great familial interests, whether royal, noble, or mercantile, not (as might be thought) to provide a conscience-saving ecclesiastical sanction to the sexual adventures of the rich. Doubtless the system was sometimes abused to this end, but there is little evidence of it.

The Divorce

The King's Chancellor, Cardinal Wolsey, also held the position of Papal legate in England; he was thus competent to give judgement on the King's cause in the Pope's name. In May 1527 he secretly began to try the case; before the proceedings were concluded, however, news reached England that the Emperor's armies had sacked Rome and made the Pope a prisoner. Catherine would have certainly appealed to Rome against any verdict given by Wolsey's court, and with the Pope a prisoner of her nephew, her appeal was likely to have been upheld. Wolsey might still have carried on regardless; but his, or Henry's, nerve did not hold. Another, more direct approach to the Pope was needed. Clement VII, however, was hardly a free agent; he was notoriously sympathetic to France, Charles's great rival. Whilst fear of a renewed Imperial assault might have held Clement from judging in Henry's favour, desire to revenge the Imperial affront might easily tell in an opposite direction. At bottom, however, these political considerations were secondary: Henry's case, once it went to Rome, would only ever be judged on its legal merits.

From the first, the most prominent opponent of Henry's case in England was John Fisher, Bishop of Rochester, a scholar of European reputation for Scriptural exegesis and more recently anti-Lutheran polemic. He wrote fully seven books on the subject of the divorce between 1527 and his death.

Henry instructed Wolsey to prepare a case, and one was prepared. Despite exhaustive consultation of obscure precedents and opinions from authorities across Europe, his case in canon law was undeniably weak. The strong consensus of opinion, backed by papal bulls and citation from the Church Fathers, was that the Levitical ban on marriage with a brother's wife was a matter not of God's or natural law (which could not be dispensed from) but simply of positive law, the law of the Church, and could (in exceptional circumstances) be dispensed from by the Pope; particularly in the case of a deceased brother's childless wife, where the text of Deuteronomy enjoins a brother to marry her to raise up children. On the ground he chose to fight, Henry was almost certain to lose[9].

Nevertheless, Wolsey persevered. His agents told the Pope bluntly that the King was in private murmuring against Papal authority; they managed to obtain a general commission for the case to be judged in England, by Wolsey and another Papal legate; but not, what he and the King desired, a decretal commission, which was a statement of the judgement to be made and authority to apply it; when one finally did arrive, its bearer (on the Pope's orders) destroyed it before it could be used. Efforts were made to persuade Catherine to enter a nunnery; she flatly refused.

The legatine court opened its hearings in Blackfriars in June 1529; Catherine at once announced she had appealed to Rome, to have the case heard there. On 16th July, the Pope granted her appeal, and revoked the case to Rome. This gave an opportunity to Wolsey's enemies at Court; he was (in October) dismissed as Lord Chancellor, and charged with praemunire (a jurisdictional offence of challenging the King's justice by wrongly asserting Papal authority). The basis of this charge was his having exercised legatine authority; we can certainly detect here an anti-Papal bias introduced by Anne Boleyn's Lutheran-sympathizing family and supporters, who unsuccessfully attempted simultaneously to confiscate much of the property of the English Church as a penalty.

Wolsey's successor as Chancellor was, unusually, a layman: Sir Thomas More.

The Breach

Although Wolsey was gone (he died before he could be tried for any of his alleged misdeeds), the business of the King's marriage remained unresolved. Diplomatic pressure was fruitless; indeed, in March 1530 Pope Clement cited Henry himself to appear in Rome for his case to be heard. In June, in a last attempt to persuade the Pope, Henry had a formal petition to grant a divorce drawn up and witnessed by six bishops, two dozen abbots, and forty-four lay peers. Thomas More, whose private opposition to the divorce was an open secret, was not asked to sign. The petition had no effect. Henry turned to another, more radical strategy.

One of the engines of Royal policy was undoubtedly the resentment of lawyers practising common law for the growing quantity of legal business (particularly the proving and execution of wills) handled by courts of Canon Law, which were typically cheaper and more efficient. It is possible to read much of this episode in English history as a working out of the long-standing tensions between the purely national body of the King's laws and the internationally accepted system of Canon Law. Certainly, disgruntled lawyers were a section of society naturally inclined to support the assertion of Royal autonomy from Rome, and one moreover heavily represented in the House of Commons. In September

1530, lawyers working for Henry put together a collection of legal precedents purporting to establish the legal autonomy of the English Church and State, under the Crown, from all external jurisdiction. This text, known as the Collectanea Satis Copiosa, heavily influenced Henry's subsequent attitude and actions.

Thomas Cromwell

In early 1531, Henry and the Boleyn faction threatened to charge the whole English clergy with praemunire for complicity in Wolsey's actions. An important figure in Henry's business was now Thomas Cromwell, one of Wolsey's men[10]. They demanded £100,000 (a vast sum) to grant a pardon. Convocation (the representative assembly of the Church in England) eventually agreed to pay this, but over five years; Henry wanted the full amount at once, pleading a threat of renewed war with France. Convocation refused, unless Henry would simultaneously legislate to define ecclesiastical privilege, especially the limits of liability for praemunire. This however was a mistake; whilst Henry needed cash, he also wanted a compliant clergy who would (if necessary) give him a divorce locally; the demanded concession would rule this out, and incorporate that ruling into English Law.

The next bill introduced for the pardon of the clergy explicitly said it was for praemunire in infringing King's

Law by appeal to Church Law. Convocation was required to state, when making its subsidy grant to fulfil its pardon, that the King was "sole protector and supreme head of the English Church and clergy", and that clerical privilege was guaranteed only inasmuch as it did not conflict with the King's law. The bishops resisted this; eventually, at the instance of John Fisher, Bishop of Rochester, the King's role as supreme head was qualified by the statement "as far as the law of God allows". With this saving clause, the Upper House of Convocation (Bishops and great abbots) admitted the statement without demur; the Lower House, and the Convocation of the Province of York, gave in only after some dissension. This of itself was not critical; the King's new title meant only what the Church allowed it to mean, which was effectively little. In its primary goal, to intimidate the Pope into conceding the divorce by threatening the English clergy, it was a complete failure.

Clement VII was more afraid of Charles V than of Henry's bluster. Cromwell and the King continued the pressure with an Annates Act, forbidding the large customary payments made by Bishops to the Pope on their appointment to a see. Passed against intense Parliamentary opposition in March 1532, it was a simple attempt to apply financial pressure to Rome. It was followed by a more important, if also more complex measure. As part of his attempt to get his legislation through the Commons, Cromwell encouraged the House to draw up a formal "Supplication" complaining of the ambition and greed of the clergy, as exemplified by the delays and expenses of clerical courts; the preamble to the text boldly claimed that Convocation, by implementing Canon Law, imposed on the laity without their consent, and trespassed on Royal prerogative. This was to make the principles of the Collectanea into a statement of policy. The Supplication was presented to the King, who read it without much enthusiasm, but proposed to mediate between the parties.

The Bishops composed a vigorous answer, asserting their traditional liberties and the independence of Canon Law. The confident tone of their text, and its implied challenge to any notion of effective Royal Supremacy, seems to have irritated Henry. On May 10th 1532, Henry demanded that Convocation concede three points: royal veto on any future canon law; making all existing canons subject to review by a mixed commission, able to strike down any it found obnoxious; and the recognition that canon law stood only because royal authority backed it. This was to demand complete surrender of the Church's legal identity and independence. Henry and his ministers exerted considerable personal and financial pressure on the Bishops; a Bill was sent to Parliament to seize the demanded concessions, should they not be made. On 15th May 1532, the Upper House of Convocation submitted; the next day, Henry accepted Thomas More's resignation as Chancellor.

Thomas Cranmer

In August, William Warham, Archbishop of Canterbury since 1503, died; in October Henry nominated as his successor Thomas Cranmer, a man of decided Lutheran sympathies and an ally of Anne Boleyn; in the same month, Anne accompanied Henry to Calais to meet the French King. By December she was pregnant; in January 1533 she and Henry secretly went through a form of marriage. Meanwhile Cromwell drafted an "appeals bill" reserving to local jurisdiction (thus removing from the competence of the Roman ecclesiastical courts) all temporal matters, including wills, tithes, and (crucially) divorces. No appeal outside England would be lawful; because, as its preamble stated "this realm of England is an empire", a unitary sovereign state subject to no higher lawful authority. The bill passed into law by April; exercising his jurisdiction within this unilaterally independent national Church, and helped by Royal pressure on Convocation, Cranmer produced in May an annulment of Henry's marriage to Catherine, and declared the Boleyn marriage lawful. She was crowned

Queen on June 1st. Within a month, Clement VII condemned the marriage, and gave Henry three months to return to Catherine under threat of excommunication. Fisher of Rochester appealed to Charles V to invade England; but in the event, the Pope drew back from excommunicating Henry, and the danger of an Imperial-led crusade passed.

In March 1534, Convocation declared that the Pope had no more authority in England than any other foreign bishop. This declaration, produced by an apparently supine attitude of Convocation at a crucial moment after years of doughty resistance to previous, lesser assaults on clerical independence, is at first sight puzzling. This sudden capitulation may be explained by persistent Royal pressure on individual Bishops: threats of praemunire, imprisonment, execution; second, a likely sense amongst many of the clergy that these measures were not, in fact, meant seriously, were little more than dumb-shows put on for a Roman audience; that this was, in sum, a purely political conflict without meaningful religious content.

This may have been the approach of the Bishops; the common run of clergy and laity were distinctly unhappy, and murmured against the move. To quell this, Parliament passed a Succession Act, requiring assent on oath to three statements: the marriage to Catherine was contrary to God's law; that between Henry and Anne was valid; and the throne should go to their issue (currently, Princess Elizabeth, born at the end of the previous year). Writing or speaking against the Boleyn marriage was treasonable. Meanwhile, the Roman court had decided the King's cause; on March 23rd the marriage was declared valid, and Henry ordered to return to Catherine.

On March 30th, the succession oath was administered to both Houses of Parliament, who assented without demur; two weeks later, to the clergy of London, who all but one took it; and to Thomas More and John Fisher, both of whom refused it, and were sent to the Tower. More certainly allowed that the King in Parliament might fix the succession where he chose; but to declare his marriage invalid was not within the competence of any except the Pope.

The Act of Supremacy

Over succeeding weeks, the oath was put to parish clergy and their parishioners across the country, and to the great religious houses. The vast majority acquiesced, although without enthusiasm: the Boleyn marriage was hardly popular. The strictest and most respected of the religious, the Carthusians and the Observant Franciscans, however, refused the oath. In December 1534, Cromwell secured the passage of two further Parliamentary measures: an Act of Supremacy declaring the King to be "the only supreme head on earth of the Church of England", and a Treasons Act declaring dissent from this opinion punishable by death.

On May 5th 1535, the priors of England's three Charterhouses - John Houghton, Robert Lawrence, and Augustine Webster - together with Richard Reynolds, a Bridgettine of Syon, for refusing the Supremacy were taken to Tyburn and butchered. They were followed by three more Carthusians on June 19th; on June 22nd John Fisher, Bishop of Rochester and recently declared a Cardinal by the Pope, was beheaded on Tower Hill. On July 6th Thomas More, after a trial in which he was convicted on perjured evidence, only after which did he declare his objections openly, was taken also to Tower Hill. There he too was beheaded: dying, he said, "in and for the faith of the Holy Catholic Church".

Popular Resistance

Henry VIII had no particular sympathy for Protestantism, although it suited his vanity (and his financial profligacy) to act as spiritual head, and disposer of the income, of the Church in England. Anne Boleyn however was a convinced Lutheran, as was her protégé Thomas Cranmer. Lutheran influence can certainly be detected in the "Ten Articles of Religion" adopted by Convocation in August 1536 (they borrowed Luther's "justification by faith" theology, and were equivocal on the sacraments), and in the simultaneous abolition of a number of saints' days.

Henry had tired of Anne by 1536; she was domineering, and had signally failed to provide a male heir (she miscarried a - probably male - child in January). She was charged, whether justly or no is difficult to say, with serial adulteries, and executed. Cranmer, who had risen to prominence as Anne Boleyn's chaplain, was instrumental in gathering evidence for her downfall. Catherine of Aragon herself died in early 1536, four months before Anne Boleyn's execution. Jane Seymour, another lady-in-waiting to both Catherine and Anne, was lined up as Henry's next wife, initially by a conservative faction opposed to religious change. Cromwell, however, was able to align himself with her cause, and bring forward more Protestant-inclined allies. One of them was Jane's brother Edward Seymour, who we will hear much more of. Whatever one's views of Henry's morals, he was at least now able to contract a canonically valid marriage; and was also, notionally, free to be reconciled with Rome. Two factors intervened: one, the Royal vanity; second, the Crown's insatiable need for ready cash.

The Suppression of the Monasteries

The largest concentration of the Church's wealth was to be found in the monasteries, which had over centuries accumulated land by bequest of the pious or guilty. In 1524, Wolsey had obtained Papal permission to suppress two dozen smaller monastic houses and use their endowments to found a new college at Oxford. Four years later, he was further permitted to suppress houses with less than a dozen residents; their revenues went to the Crown. This still left more than eight hundred monastic houses throughout England, collective masters of enormous landed wealth. As part of the Annates Act of 1534, Cromwell had carried out a comprehensive survey of the property of the English Church. This document, the Valor Ecclesiasticus, was invaluable in what followed. In 1536, on the pretence that the smaller houses lacked the resources properly to follow their rule, Royal commissioners inspected a small proportion of them and, on flimsy evidence, concluded that they were as a body irretrievably lax and scandalous. They were accordingly dissolved by Act of Parliament, and their property annexed to the Crown. This provision affected over four hundred houses. The majority of the monks and nuns either accepted nominal pensions, or requested transfer to other larger houses (these transfers typically never happened). The evidence of irregular living collected by the commissioners is highly suspect; at best, it may represent the type of internal gossip invariable in religious communities; at worst, simple invention practised for gain. The Crown's need for immediate money was so acute that a large proportion of former monastic land was quickly alienated at bargain prices.

The Pilgrimage of Grace

Suppressing the monasteries was clearly profoundly shocking to the country at large, particularly in the north. Isolated protests soon turned into a full-scale rebellion - known at the time, and to history, as the Pilgrimage of Grace. Underlying it were complex causes varying from place to place, including economic factors; but the primary and unifying motive was undoubtedly religious protest against suppression of monasteries and the presence of heretical bishops (such as Cranmer) and low-

born Royal counsellors (such as Cromwell); not to
mention the objectionable "Ten Articles" of belief. By the
end of 1536, upwards of 40,000 men led by Robert Aske,
a Yorkshire lawyer, had gathered under the banner of the
Five Wounds of Christ. Royal government and religious
policy in the north of England became impossible. Aske
however was designedly moderate, and on the King's
promise of a general pardon and a Parliament to consider
their grievances, he persuaded his followers to disperse.
Henry had no intention of keeping his word; a further
smaller rising in January 1537 gave him the excuse to
arrest and execute Aske and others, and for Royal troops
easily (and savagely) to scatter and suppress their
leaderless followers. The Pilgrimage of Grace could most
certainly have brought down the King, or at least his
ministers, in 1536 had not its leaders been restrained and
loyal. As it was, it gave an object lesson to those opposed
to Henry on the perils of that opposition.

In 1539, a renewed financial crisis brought the final
suppression of the remaining, greater monasteries.
Cromwell and Henry successfully obscured the meaning
of this attack by promising to refound them as secular
colleges or cathedrals; a promise ignored, of course -of a
hundred and fifty larger monasteries, only six became
Cathedrals, but stripped of most of their endowments;
eight of the existing Cathedrals were staffed by monastic

chapters, who became secular canons. The remainder of the monasteries were destroyed, including the great pilgrimage sites of Walsingham and Glastonbury, or stripped of valuables (like the famous shrine of Thomas à Becket in Canterbury).

Vested Interests

It does not seem likely, as has been suggested, that the desire to seize monastic wealth was in itself a reason for Henry's breach with Rome; but it was an undoubtedly convenient by-product. Suppression of the monasteries had, moreover, critical economic and political consequences: much land was quickly alienated from the Crown by need to raise ready money; this (a process accelerated under Edward VI) soon produced a substantial class of "new men", adventurers and arriviste functionaries whose fortune and position was thus directly founded on the downfall of traditional religion. They therefore had a strong interest in avoiding any reconciliation with Rome, and also formed a counterweight both to the authority of the Crown, and to that of the old landed nobility. This body of men held high office under Henry and his successors, supplanting the old magnates (the Nevilles, Percys, Howards, Poles), and provided a Protestant aristocratic class who evolved into the Whig oligarchy who largely governed England for the next four centuries. The roll-call of these men's names - Cecil, Cromwell, Russell, Cavendish, Seymour, Spencer -marks a new and durable force in the political and religious history of England. Edward Seymour's position in particular was cemented after the birth, in October 1537, of a son, also named Edward, to Henry's new Queen, his sister; she died soon after the birth.

Other consequences of the dissolution are less quantifiable; the disruption to the social fabric by the removal of the substantial practical charities of the religious foundations must have been considerable; whilst the sheer aesthetic loss of buildings, painting and woodcarving, metal and jewel-work, not to mention the vast numbers of manuscripts destroyed, is simply incalculable, but can only be accounted a cultural, educational and literary disaster. The surviving fragments of England's medieval artistic heritage can only hint at the magnitude of our loss.

In the same year, 1539, as saw the end of the great monasteries, Henry introduced the Six Articles of Religion. These, an official statement of the English Church's doctrine, defend traditional practices - transubstantiation, private masses, clerical celibacy, auricular confession - and were to be valid until Edward VI's majority. Archbishop Cranmer was obliged to send his wife, whom he had married secretly, back home to

Germany. The general tenor of Henry's policy for the remainder of his reign is distinctly traditional, orthodox even. Cromwell's hopes of allying England with German Lutherans came to nothing; his promotion of Henry's fourth marriage, to the German Anne of Cleves (whose sister was wife to the arch-Protestant Elector of Saxony) led in 1540 to his downfall and death.

In the summer of 1546, Henry was negotiating with Pope Paul III about acknowledging papal supremacy, and was willing to submit his case to the soon to be called Council of Trent. Had Henry died in the autumn of 1546, his son's Regency would have been governed by the conservative bishops Gardiner and Tunstall, and the great lay magnate the Duke of Norfolk. All their instincts would have led to an eventual reconciliation with Rome. But nothing came of this; Henry did not die, but his health deteriorated further. Unable to write, his signature was affixed to documents with an inked stamp. Real power passed to his Protestant advisers led by Edward Seymour, John Dudley[11] and Cranmer. They strictly controlled access to the King, and what documents were issued in his name. The conservative faction at court was defeated; Norfolk was first removed from the projected Council of Regency and then sent with his son to the Tower. His son was executed; Norfolk himself was only saved by the King's death. It is abundantly clear that

Henry had no desire to see England a Protestant country, but events were no longer in his hands.

Edward VI and Queen Mary

In January 1547 Henry died, aged only fifty-five, obese and enfeebled, his health undermined by excess and by numerous injuries sustained on the hunting field and the tournament ground[12]. His nine year old son by Jane Seymour became Edward VI. Seymour, the new King's uncle, was created Duke of Somerset and Lord Protector - King in all but name until Edward's majority. Like many around the new King, Somerset had profited largely from monastic suppression; intellectual conviction aside, he and his supporters had a strong vested interest in cementing the breach with Rome, since any restitution of Church lands would hit them financially very hard. Somerset was in correspondence with John Calvin, who advised him on the best way to implement Protestantism. The young King himself had been educated by tutors whose extreme Calvinist sympathies were perhaps not entirely known to Henry, but which had taken root. The Somerset regency soon moved to dismantle the semi-detached Catholicism of Henry's later years. In the summer of 1547, Injunctions were issued ordering images to be destroyed, prohibiting feast and fast days, the use of the Rosary, the burning of lights in Church except for two on the altar, and all religious processions whatever. In September, parish visitations began to enforce these changes. Parliament met in November, and (albeit with strong opposition) repealed Henry's Six Articles of Religion; since Somerset wielded the extensive powers of Crown patronage and enforcement, neither House was inclined to be other than eventually compliant. The following month, a Chantries Act suppressed all chantry chapels and similar small foundations established to offer prayers for the dead. This also abolished most charitable colleges, hospitals, and fraternities. Henry had suppressed a few such foundations two years previously, but left the principle untouched. This Act had a dual purpose, or at least effect: a religious one, inasmuch as it was an explicit attack on the doctrine of Purgatory and prayer for the dead, and by implication on the whole notion of the value of works in religion; and a financial, since the Crown appropriated both whatever plate and other physical appurtenances belonged to the chantry foundations, and also annexed the very considerable capital sums with which they were endowed for the maintenance of the priests who served them. This led to another effect, this time a social one: perhaps ten thousand clergy were employed as chantry priests; this Act made them at a stroke unemployed. As well as their duties of prayer, chantry priests had typically assisted with the ministry of their local parish, and were often obliged to teach the young and look after the sick and aged. Former chantry priests were allowed nominal pensions from the Crown; many, perhaps most, of them continued their ministry informally; but their official role and social function disappeared, and as they diminished by natural wastage, their numbers were not renewed. Chantries had received regular bequests from all ranks of society until the end of Henry's reign; indeed, he himself had left £600 in his will to endow masses for his soul in perpetuity. These provisions, like all others, were abrogated by the Act. Clergy recruitment fell almost to nothing; education and charitable works at a local level were massively disrupted.

The Book of Common Prayer

During 1548, commissioners spread out across the country to enforce religious change, destroying images, confiscating church plate, suppressing processions and the panoply of ceremonies and customs familiar to the Catholic people. There was sporadic resistance by crowds of aggrieved parishioners in Cornwall, Sussex, Hampshire, and across the South of England; some offered violence to the commissioners, and were met with savage reprisal.

Somerset's government was not abashed, and (in January 1549) passed the Uniformity Act, which abolished the (Latin) Mass and replaced it by the

(English) Book of Common Prayer, a compromise text whose original extreme Protestantism had been slightly modified to appease conservative elements. When the Act came into force in June, there was widespread rioting across the country; in Devon and Cornwall, insurgents rose in rebellion, and Exeter was besieged. In each case the motive behind the resistance was specifically religious - people wanted the Mass back. The risings (sometimes called the "Prayer-Book Rebellion") were not co-ordinated, however, and were suppressed piecemeal; in August Lord Russell led a royal force, stiffened with Italian mercenaries, against the Western Rising, which was suppressed with much slaughter. Russell was made Earl of Bedford for his pains.

Nevertheless the shock of the revolts, and his stubborn prosecution of war with Scotland, brought Somerset down. For some months the balance of power was unclear; conservative peers and bishops edged towards power, but were eventually once more sidelined. Somerset's sidekick John Dudley, now Earl of Warwick (and soon to become Duke of Northumberland), assumed control as Lord President of the Council. Somerset was sent to the Tower, and three years later was beheaded. In the same year, a statute permitted the clergy to marry. At the most generous estimate, no more than fifteen per cent - one in seven - of the clergy took wives during this period.

Liturgical Reforms

Despite the dismal reception of the 1549 Prayer Book (even where it was put into use, priests deliberately gave the service a ceremonial and ritual colouring as close to the old Mass as the text would permit, to the dismay of Cranmer, Ridley and others) Dudley and his cronies pressed ahead. In March 1550, a new Ordinal was published, which in place of the former rite of ordaining priests had a pared down and Protestantized version compiled on the advice of Martin Bucer, a German ex-Dominican turned extreme reformer now holding the Regius chair of Divinity at Cambridge. It is generally agreed to express a deficient understanding of the Catholic doctrine of Holy Orders[13].

At the same time, Ridley and others began a campaign to remove altars from churches, and replace them with communion tables. There was considerable reluctance in most places, and amongst many Bishops; in November, the Council gave this change the force of law. Gradually, too, such conservative Bishops as were left from Henry's reign (including Gardiner and Tunstall) were deprived or imprisoned, and replaced by energetically Protestant figures. Between 1550 and 1553 much of the landed property of the old sees was seized by the Crown, to repair the again tottering Royal finances.

Catholic opposition to these measures tended to rally around the Lady Mary, the King's half-sister, Catherine of Aragon's daughter. She was forced to accept the Supremacy, but otherwise protected by the interest of the Spanish crown. Her sympathies were not hidden; in May 1551, at the height of Ridley's campaign against the "superstition" of the Rosary, she had ridden through London with one hundred and thirty knights, gentlemen, and ladies, each carrying a large set of Rosary beads.

Liturgical reform also continued. Cranmer considered the 1549 Prayer Book to be no more than a stopping point along the road to a properly reformed communion service. Taking advice from Bucer, and the Italian Zwinglian Peter Martyr (now holding the Regius chair at Oxford), he composed a new and more radical Book of Common Prayer, which included a Communion Service deliberately unlike the Mass, with a Eucharistic theology explicitly opposed to the Real Presence of Christ in the sacrament, instead adopting Calvin's theories that the eucharist was no more than a spiritual memorial. This text was imposed by another Act of Uniformity in 1552; its reception in the parishes was even less enthusiastic than the 1549 version, although this time there were no significant popular disturbances. The following year, the theology of the reformers' Church of England was first spelled out, in the Forty Two Articles of Religion. Subscription to them was required of all clergy, schoolmasters, and members of the universities proceeding to take their degrees. They openly denied Catholic teaching on transubstantiation, purgatory, invocation of the saints, and the place of good works in religion; their general tenor is Calvinist. We cannot really tell how these Articles would have been received, for they were never properly implemented; a month after they were promulgated, Edward VI, always a sickly boy, was dead, aged fifteen.

Unpopularity of Reform

What we can determine, however, is the general attitude of the country to these innovations. It was almost without exception unenthusiastic, tending to hostile. Moreover, these official assaults on accepted custom and practice tended to provoke not simply outright hostility, but a general indifference to religion. Parish finances are in terrible shape across the country, as legacies to the support of the Church go into sharp decline, and the income previously derived from parish ales, sheep and similar customs vanish as these are abolished. Recruitment to the clergy falls almost to nothing. In the last two years of Edward's reign, persistent (and accurate) rumours that the Crown was planning systematically to seize valuable Church plate led to widespread pre-emptive dispersal of this and other parish assets. Some of this was eventually returned; much was not. When the order for confiscation was at last issued, it was met with general obstruction and concealment. Northumberland's government had managed to make itself remarkably unpopular, on grounds of simple religious principle. Not that attempts to convince the people otherwise had been lacking; numerous Protestant preachers had toured particularly the south and south-east of England, and had (as later evidence proves) made a number of converts to their gospel of "lively faith", and contempt for Papist superstitions; but their followers (distinct from those who tolerated them out of deference or intimidation) were vanishingly few in number.

In Luther's Germany, what had begun as a religious quarrel had taken on political resonance and meaning; in England, the reverse is true. Henry's breach with Rome was a purely political action; only later, and particularly under Edward and later Elizabeth, does it assume a religious colouring, and that almost by accident. In Germany, a religious dispute was hijacked by unscrupulous political factions; in England, Protestant sectaries seized the occasion of a political upheaval to impose their religious agenda.

Queen Mary

On Edward's death, 6th July 1553, Northumberland moved fast. He had chosen the fifteen-year-old Lady Jane Grey, a great-granddaughter of Henry VII, and his own daughter-in-law, to be Queen. She was a convinced and articulate Protestant. Northumberland despatched troops, led by his son Robert (later Earl of Leicester, and Elizabeth's favourite) to arrest the Lady Mary at her house in Hertfordshire. She had been forewarned, however, and had left in the night of 4th July, making her way in secret via houses of her supporters to Kenninghall in Norfolk. There she wrote to the Council claiming the throne as her father's daughter and in accordance with his will. Her prospects seemed slim; Northumberland was safe in London, and in control of the considerable military and financial power of the Crown. He had Jane Grey proclaimed Queen throughout the country. In Suffolk, however, the commons proclaimed Queen Mary. She based herself in Framlingham Castle, and wrote to her supporters asking for help. From across southern England, the gentry and nobility and their tenants rallied to her; the Earl of Derby and Lord Dacre marched their retainers down from the north to join her. Everywhere the common people refused to acclaim Jane Grey, or enlist in the levies Northumberland was raising on her behalf. Northumberland was dismayed at Mary's gathering support. Upwards of 20,000 men flocked to her standard in Framlingham. She then moved on London. Northumberland himself led out a small force - the six hundred men of the royal guard, and some hundreds of cavalry - and met Mary's army at Bury St Edmunds. By now, she had perhaps 30,000 men; Northumberland's expected reinforcements had not arrived. He retreated to Cambridge where, on 20th July, he was arrested and taken to the Tower. Jane Grey and her husband were also imprisoned there. Mary entered London to popular rejoicing.

Restoring Catholicism

From the beginning of August, Mass was said unofficially by priests across the country; on August 18th the Queen expressed the wish that her subjects would follow her religious lead. Altars were widely rebuilt, and Masses (still formally illegal) became widespread. In December, the Protestant legislation brought in by Somerset over Edward's name was repealed, opposed by a minority of the House of Commons; another act re-established the Mass as the only legal form of worship in time for Christmas. There was some local delay in implementing the restoration, but for the most part the old rites were celebrated with enthusiasm and the apparatus of Protestantism thrown out. The one thing lacking was the formal absolution of the realm from schism. This task was delegated by the Pope, Julius III, to the Queen's cousin, Reginald Cardinal Pole; his arrival in England was delayed by the need for Papal approval for exempting those who had obtained monastic and other Church property from the duty of restoring it. Without this concession, Mary's advisers knew the substantial landed interests would resist being reconciled; eventually the Pope gave way. On 20th November 1554, Cardinal Pole formally absolved both Houses of Parliament, and the whole realm with them, from heresy and schism. Many of the assembled Lords and Commons publicly wept as they received the absolution. Again, on December 2nd, a vast crowd after solemn High Mass knelt at St Paul's Cross and were in tears absolved.

Mary's policy of restoration was overwhelmingly popular and successful. A good indicator of this is the speed with which the appurtenances of Catholic worship - mass books, an altar, rood, images of patron saints - were reintroduced after the destructions of the previous reign. Despite a hard economic climate, and the considerable expense, the vast majority of parishes across the country restored these elements within two years of her accession. In contrast with the reluctance and resistance met by Protestantizing reforms under Henry and Edward, the hallmark of the Marian Church is the enthusiasm and generosity with which the changes were implemented at the parish level. Little encouragement or enforcement from above was needed to revive Catholic worship; contemporary wills show an immediate increase in giving to the Church. There was a substantial increase, too, in the numbers coming forward for ordination. Moreover Reginald Pole had definite and detailed plans for the thorough reform of the moral and financial condition of the English clergy, including the foundation of seminaries on the Tridentine model. In 1555 he convoked the Synod of London, which formally initiated this process.

'Alienating' the people

One of the most persistent aspects of the "official history" of this period is the claim that Mary destroyed her initial popularity, and forever alienated the English people from Catholicism, in three ways. First, she married the King of Spain; second, she at his instance began an unpopular and disastrous war with France, which ended with the loss of Calais, England's last possession on the continent; third, she gave life to the Protestant cause, and exposed the true savagery of papistry, by burning large numbers of people as heretics, including the sometime Bishops Cranmer, Latimer, and Ridley, who all became martyrs for the cause of English religion.

None of this is true. The Spanish marriage was in fact widely popular. When Mary's intention to marry Philip became clear, in November 1553, a Parliamentary delegation urged her to reconsider. When she ignored it, more active plotting began; this resulted in a number of attempted rebellions in January of the following year. Of these, all were stillborn except for one raised in Kent by Sir Thomas Wyatt, who managed to gather some three thousand men by dint of spreading misleading rumours of Spanish invasions, and protestations of loyalty to Mary (in fact he intended to depose her in favour of Elizabeth, almost certainly with the latter's knowledge and collusion). The rebellion was crushed with ease, and signally failed to gain popular support despite inflammatory rhetoric.

Whatever the attitude of the newly enriched gentry to a Catholic royal marriage, popular opinion was in favour. As for the second point: war with France had been for centuries more normal than not, with or without Spanish allies; the loss of Calais was a blow, certainly, but not an insuperable one; besides, when has fighting the French ever been unpopular amongst Englishmen? Third, and most importantly, the execution of heretics (some three hundred or so in all) was for the nation as a whole a matter for either approval or indifference. In London, perhaps, and some parts of East Anglia, there was some

sympathy for those burnt, together with admiration for
the bravery with which some met their deaths; however
heretics were generally unpopular, usually identified by,
and convicted on the evidence of, their neighbours, and of
negligible influence on the opinions of society at large.
The hagiographic pieties of John Foxe's 1563 Acts and
Monuments ("Foxe's Book of Martyrs"), which describes
those who died under Mary together with a very
heterogeneous collection of late medieval dissenters, are
emphatically not representative of contemporary views,
but rather of the sophisticated mechanics of Elizabethan
propaganda. The majority of those dissatisfied with
Mary's religious policy (a tiny minority of the population
except in some urban centres) either silently conformed,
or (like Foxe) went into exile.

Succession

There was discontent in the country, for certain, but largely
because of rising food prices caused by a series of bad
harvests; an epidemic of influenza in 1558 made recruiting
for the army difficult, particularly given recent reverses.
The most pressing problem, however, was Mary's
successor. Her closest legitimate heir was Mary Stuart,
Queen of Scots. She was politically unacceptable as an ally
of France, and indeed Queen of a country itself at war with
England. A case could have been made for Cardinal Pole,

but his claim (via his mother, daughter of Edward IV's younger brother the Duke of Clarence) derived from the Yorkist line and would have reawoken the danger of dynastic dispute and civil war. Mary seems to have placed her hopes in a child of her own (she had an apparent phantom pregnancy in 1554-5); Elizabeth's claim she was reluctant even to recognize, for apart from her official bastardy as the child of an adulterous union (this could have been papally dispensed from) there is some evidence that Mary, and others, believed her father to have been not Henry but one of Anne Boleyn's lovers. The critical factor seems to have been the support for Elizabeth's candidacy by Mary's husband, Philip II of Spain - and this despite her almost certain involvement in Wyatt's rebellion, and her consequent house arrest at Woodstock.

Mary Stuart would have meant an Anglo-French alignment, inevitably hostile to Spanish interests; moreover, Elizabeth had publicly conformed to Catholic practice throughout Mary's reign, and there was no reason to think she would change her religious attitude. The Queen's health visibly declined during 1558. Believing herself to be pregnant, and afraid of dying in childbirth, she left instructions in her will (which does not mention Elizabeth, although Mary apparently assented verbally to her succession) for Philip II to be regent during her child's minority. In fact she very likely had uterine or ovarian cancer, and died on 17th November 1558. Cardinal Pole, Archbishop of Canterbury since the previous year, died some twelve hours later. Mary's death was unexpected, and (like all the Tudor monarchs) untimely; for Catholicism in England, it was disastrous.

Elizabeth I

Almost the first act of Elizabeth's reign was to appoint to her Council a number of convinced Protestants, formerly in power under Edward VI, led by William Cecil. Cecil first rose to prominence under Edward as secretary to Somerset (Seymour); transferring his allegiance to the elder Dudley (Northumberland), he was instrumental in Somerset's fall, and was rewarded by Dudley with the post of Secretary to the Council. Like most of the principal players in Edward's reformation, he amassed considerable riches. Under Mary, he apparently conformed to Catholic practice; he was in touch with Elizabeth before Mary's death, and was instrumental in smoothing her accession. He assumed the post of Secretary of State - effectively ruling the country - and retained it until 1572, when he became Lord High Treasurer. He held this place until his death in 1598[14].

The practical results of this were almost immediate, and are generally known as "the Elizabethan Settlement". This was a series of Acts of Parliament passed in 1559, some slightly modified later in her reign, establishing the form of religious practice permitted throughout the realm. They are often described by historians of Anglicanism as a splendid compromise between the excesses of, on the one hand, Edwardian Protestant extremism, and Marian Catholicism on the other. In fact, they were undisguisedly Protestant in intention and effect. The Elizabethan settlement can be said to "compromise" with Catholicism only if that word can bear the sense of "defame, proscribe, attempt legally to extirpate", a sense unknown to the makers of dictionaries. The 1559 Act of Supremacy imposed the Queen as "supreme governor" of Church of England in matters both spiritual and temporal and, like its equivalent under Edward, its attestation was required of all holding public office, teaching in schools, or proceeding to university degrees; an Act of Uniformity in the same year prescribed the exclusive use of a very slightly modified version of Cranmer's 1552 Prayer Book, and the Ordinal of Edward VI. The Mass was in effect banned; hearing Mass even privately was an offence, whilst failure to attend the prescribed Prayer Book service was punishable by a fine of 12d for each instance[15].

All but one of those who had been Bishops under Mary refused the Act of Supremacy, and were deprived of their sees. Some fled abroad; the rest were imprisoned. They were replaced by men of decided Protestant temper, some extreme. Pole's place as Archbishop of Canterbury was taken by Matthew Parker, an obscure Cambridge don once Anne Boleyn's chaplain[16]. Whatever Elizabeth's own views (and she seems to have been in matters of religion very much her mother's daughter) she (or Cecil) needed clergy willing to run an avowedly national church; the only men who would do so were by definition convinced Protestants, and it is this practical reason, as much as any conscientious conviction on her part, that determines the thoroughgoing Protestantism of her "settlement".

Nor was it just the Bishops who refused to conform; substantial numbers of parish clergy resigned, went abroad, or took up a fugitive existence as tutors, chaplains, schoolmasters, and said Mass in secret. Over a hundred Fellows of Oxford and Cambridge Colleges resigned their Fellowships and went abroad, where they formed the nucleus of a very active and prolific body of exiled Catholic intellectuals.

The Thirty-Nine Articles

The measures of 1559 did not finish things. In 1563 were prefaced to the Prayer Book Thirty-Eight Articles of Religion, drawn largely from the 1552 Lutheran Augsburg Confession submitted to the Council of Trent, but modified so as to admit a more radical Calvinist interpretation. Eventually (in 1571) they assumed final form as Thirty-Nine Articles, and remain the official statement of belief of the Church of England. They contain explicit denials of, inter alia, Purgatory, prayer to the Saints, the use of images, the sacraments except baptism and the Eucharist, the Real Presence of Christ in the consecrated elements (not simply the mechanism of transubstantiation), clerical celibacy, and the jurisdiction of the Pope; no Catholic could possibly accept them, or (other than by remarkable sleight of hand) suppose them capable of a Catholic interpretation[17]. In the following century, subscription to these articles was required of any holding public office; during Elizabeth's reign, this was only required of ordained clergy. Nevertheless they had the effect of making the Anglican Church the preserve of an exclusively, even aggressively Protestant ministry. The equivocations possible under Henry or Edward could no longer be made. The convinced, and in many cases extreme Protestants now holding all the English and Welsh Bishoprics intended to ensure that their clergy's attitude to Catholicism was equally uncompromising. The "Elizabethan Settlement", in fact, is a convenient myth hiding increasing intolerance of Catholic practice.

Catholic Uprising

In November 1569, the Earls of Northumberland and Westmorland (heads of the traditionally powerful Percy and Neville families) entered Durham Cathedral with seventy men and overthrew the apparatus of the new Protestant worship (the communion table and the service books). The following day, they proclaimed an open rebellion in the cause of restoring the Catholic religion. Whilst their personal motives may have been mixed (both had been denied preferment by Cecil's government) the six thousand or more from the northern counties who soon joined them were predominantly impelled by desire for the old religion. They marched south behind the old badge of the Pilgrimage of Grace, the banner of the Five Wounds, with the aim of freeing Mary Stuart from Tutbury Castle and making her Queen. Meanwhile Protestant service books were destroyed across the north, and the Mass widely restored. When the Earls reached Leeds, however, they learned that Mary Stuart had been moved to Coventry, which their army was too weak to take by storm. They retreated northwards, and took Hartlepool, in the hope that Spanish troops might be landed there, and appealed for further local support. But the Earls had struck too soon; they asked the Pope for a statement of support, but it did not arrive in time. Nor did the substantial Catholic population of Lancashire and much of Yorkshire join them, unsure of the legitimacy of rebellion against their sovereign. A royal army was raised in the Midlands; as it marched north, it was not resisted, and a week before Christmas, the Earls fled to Scotland. Those who had joined them suffered the usual savage Tudor response to treason. This marks the last throw of the once great feudal power of the old magnates of the north; henceforth, no great nobleman of old family is willing or able to venture his fortunes against the growing strength of central, and Protestant, authority.

Excommunication of Elizabeth I

This rising had other unfortunate consequences for English Catholics. The Pope did in the event issue a Bull declaring Elizabeth heretic and excommunicate, and absolving her subjects from their allegiance. His immediate prompt for doing so seems to have been the Earls' rising; the grounds for doing so were straightforward: she was illegitimate, had violated her coronation oath (made to a Catholic Bishop) to maintain the Church, had deposed bishops, issued an heretical Prayer Book, and denied her subjects the Sacraments. The Bull did not reach England, however, until early in 1570, when the Earls' rising had already failed. Its publication[18] was precisely the excuse Cecil's regime needed. Enforcement of the recusancy laws became immediately fiercer.

In 1574 Francis Walsingham, another returned Protestant exile who had been one of William Cecil's fixers throughout the reign, became Secretary to the Council, and master of an extensive network of spies and double agents charged with subverting notional threats to the Crown. First on the list of suspects were English recusant Catholics; the history of the next few decades is riddled with the convoluted stratagems of agents provocateurs. One of the regular features of this period is the discovery of "plots", typically aiming at the life of the Queen, demonstrably encouraged and enabled by Walsingham's agents with the aim of implicating such as he wished to remove[19].

The Age of Martyrs

1574 also saw the arrival of the first "seminary priests", ordained from amongst the Catholic exiles at colleges in Douai and Rome; they were joined by Jesuits six years later. Something like six hundred priests came to England on the mission before 1603. Counter-reformation standards finally penetrate into English Church with these seminary priests and Jesuits. Royal policy had previously been one of passive waiting for obstinately Catholic clergy, survivors of Mary's reign, to die off, and adherence thus to perish by inanition. With this infusion of new priests, the Government moved to active persecution.

The first of them to be caught and executed was Cuthbert Mayne, in 1577. He, like others martyred in the first years of the mission, was convicted on a supposed charge of publishing a papal bull in England, which after Regnans in Excelsis was treasonable. This need for a concrete charge was an impediment to Cecil and Walsingham, however; from 1581, it was high treason to reconcile or be reconciled to the Catholic Church, the primary activity and purpose of the missionary priests. Another Act in 1585 made it high treason for any priest ordained abroad to enter the country; to harbour such a one was a felony. High treason was punished by the peculiarly brutal death of hanging, drawing, and quartering. Several hundred Catholics, priests and laity alike, were executed under these statutes before the end of Elizabeth's reign. Their names still have resonance: Edmund Campion, Robert Southwell, John Southworth, Margaret Clitherow, Ralph Sherwin, and so many others. We may call this the heroic age of English Catholicism.

Underground Catholics

As the official formularies of Elizabethan religion were gradually implemented, and the old Marian clergy were replaced by the products of the reformed Universities, the public face of English religion became visibly more Protestant. This led to a distinct growth in the numbers of "underground" Catholics throughout the 1570's; with the renewed severity of persecution in the 1580's, however, and despite the best efforts of the missionary clergy, many were driven to conform. This persecution was marked with all the characteristics of state terror familiar to students of twentieth century history: informers, confiscations of property, deprivation of civil rights, imprisonment, torture, disinformation. All that was required to avoid this was conformity to the state-sponsored form of religion. The persecution was officially justified by characterizing Catholicism as inherently treasonous, because of its implicit obedience to the Pope, seen as a foreign monarch. Given the support of the Spanish Hapsburgs for English Catholic exiles, this assumption could be made; certainly, both William Cardinal Allen, de facto leader of the exiled clergy, and Robert Parsons, senior English Jesuit, encouraged political schemes to return England to the Faith; but the majority of the exiles, and those who returned as missionary priests, demonstrably had no aim except the religious one of encouraging constancy in recusants and reconciling those who had conformed.

These were themselves political acts, in the eyes of a state that claimed allegiance over men's consciences and worship. Some of the exiles did try to take things further; Dr Nicolas Sander, sometime Fellow of New College Oxford and author of a polemical and highly-coloured history, The Rise and Growth of the Anglican Schism, is an instance of a definitely political Catholicism. He went to Ireland in 1579 as Papal agent, with the aim of fomenting rebellion, and died, unsuccessful, two years later.

Mary Queen of Scots

Insofar as most Catholics hoped for a political solution to their misfortunes, however, they looked to Mary Stuart. Mary Stuart - Mary Queen of Scots - had taken refuge in England in 1568, aged twenty-six, after a Calvinist-led rebellion inspired in part by her own misgovernment and chronic favouritism. She was Catholic, and (as a great-grand-daughter of Henry VII) a legitimate claimant to the throne of England; in fact, after the death of Cardinal Pole, she was heir presumptive to Mary. After Regnans in Excelsis in 1570 released English Catholics from allegiance to Elizabeth, Mary Stuart was arguably rightful Queen of England.

For almost twenty years she was effectively held prisoner; as the condition of Catholics in England worsened, she became the focus of hopes and aspirations. She was too valuable to be let loose; too important to be killed out of hand. The treason legislation of 1585 made it a capital offence for anyone with any claim to the throne to be privy to, or complicit in, any plot against the life of the sovereign. This was transparently aimed at Mary Stuart. In order to condemn her, however, Walsingham needed a conspiracy for her to become acquainted with. He briskly set about devising one. This was the so-called Babington Plot. Double-agents were insinuated into Mary's circle, and encouraged her to use a supposedly secret message system (via beer barrels) that was in fact being read by Walsingham. His agents then egged on a hot-headed young Catholic nobleman, known to Mary, one Anthony Babington, to some loose talk about killing Elizabeth, which he was prevailed on to put in a letter to Mary. Under the 1585 Act, this was enough to kill her; a suspicious postscript to one of her letters to Babington (she claimed it was forged) approving the attempt put the seal on it. Mary Stuart was executed on 8th February 1587.

Philip of Spain

The other main hope of Catholics was external to England, and lay in the action of Philip of Spain, once (as husband to Mary Tudor) himself King of England. He was indefatigable in the Catholic cause, not only when it coincided with Spanish interests; he was centrally concerned in the decisive victory of the Christian fleet over Muslim Turkish aggression at Lepanto in 1571. As early as 1573, egged on by English Catholic exiles, he had made a solemn treaty with the Pope to reconvert England. Throughout the 1570s and 80s, Spanish influence was sought in a vain effort to alleviate the worst of the penal laws.

Meanwhile, Philip was increasingly annoyed and inconvenienced by English disruption of the bullion shipments from his dominions in the New World, by the quasi-piratical actions (unofficially encouraged by Cecil) of freebooters such as John Hawkins and Francis Drake, and by English support for Dutch rebels against Spanish rule in the Low Countries[20]. This support became official in 1585 with the Treaty of Nonsuch between England and the rebellious Dutch "United Provinces"; England was now formally at war with Spain. English support was critical for the maintenance of the Dutch rebellion. Philip of Spain began to collect a fleet to attack England.

His general frustrations were given added point by the execution of Mary Stuart, an act widely shocking to most European monarchies. She had, moreover, by her will left her own claim to the English throne in the hands of Philip. He obtained Papal authority to depose Elizabeth and replace her with whomsoever he chose. It is unlikely, however, that in preparing his fleet (known to history as "the Spanish Armada") he intended a full-scale conquest of England, which would have been difficult with Spanish resources already stretched by the Dutch campaign; rather, Philip's aims were likely to have been, most importantly, the end of aid to the Dutch and interference in the bullion shipments; and a measure of toleration for English Catholics. Replacing Elizabeth would have been difficult since, with Mary Stuart dead, there was no obvious Catholic candidate with a plausible claim. Nevertheless, the religious motive was certainly present in Philip's mind.

In the event the Armada was foiled by vigorous English naval action, and then suffered substantial loss in appalling storms in the North Sea and the Atlantic. Elizabethan and subsequent propaganda presented this as a symbolic victory for Protestant arms; this overstates the case very considerably. The core of the Spanish fleet survived; English attempts to destroy it in harbour the following year met with disaster. The war with Spain dragged on until 1604, largely to England's disadvantage.

How Catholic was England under Elizabeth?

We have here an extreme difficulty of accurately measuring allegiance. At Elizabeth's accession in 1558, the vast majority of the country was definitely Catholic in both sympathy and practice. By 1603, at the end of her reign, the numbers, if we only count "official" recusants, are quite small: there were roughly nine thousand registered recusants throughout the country.

This figure is however an enormous underestimate, for several reasons. Undoubtedly local sympathies could readily lead to fines not being collected, or non-attendance at the parish church ignored. In some places the boundaries were unclear; priests ordained under Mary used the new books, but celebrated in a fashion as like the old Mass as possible; or held "underground" Masses in addition to the Prayer Book service, often to much the same congregation. Eventually, however, such priests died, or were delated and deprived of their livings.

Then there are sympathizers, or nominal conformists, who for fear or from whatever social or personal pressure attended the parish church occasionally, but were wholly Catholic in sympathy (these "Church Papists" were likely very numerous); then there were those Catholic in background or allegiance (like

Shakespeare) who for reasons of ambition and career compounded with the state religion. Christopher Haigh writes: "It is likely that most of those who lived in Tudor England experienced Reformation as obedience rather than conversion; they obeyed a monarch's new laws rather than swallowed a preacher's new message"[21].

The pace of implementing state-imposed reformed religion was fitful, and in many places obstinately slow: some parishes, reluctant to concede that Protestantism was permanent, did not re-order their churches, or throw out Mass vestments, until Elizabeth had reigned thirty years or more.

Nevertheless these repeated state efforts to enforce varying religious conformity had two effects: first, to increase the number of those who regarded religion with indifference or cynicism, as something to be done from time to time for social reasons, but whose ultimate form was (because so often changed) unimportant; and second, paradoxically and conversely, for persecution to sharpen the awareness of religious difference, and the value of conscientious adherence to it, particularly amongst dissenting groups - whether Protestants under Mary or Catholics and the ultra-Protestant fringes the rest of the time.

Meanwhile the Universities, converted into Protestant academies after the resignation or flight of a substantial proportion of Catholic fellows, produced large numbers of convinced Protestant preachers who assumed the duties of parish clergy as those ordained under Mary died or went underground. Their efforts at evangelizing the laity combined with the vigorous action of Protestant bishops, and the eclipse of many of the great Catholic noble houses (epitomized by the failure of the rising of the northern Earls), to foster a real allegiance to Protestant ideas amongst a vocal minority of the population, and a sullen acquiescence in them on the part of the majority.

Active Catholicism, particularly as the old Marian priests died off in the 1580s, became increasingly confined to marginal enclaves (Lancashire, parts of Yorkshire and Wales, the Marches) and to the houses, dependants and tenants of the recusant nobility and gentry, who were able to offer both a measure of legal protection and (more importantly) access to the sacraments by giving refuge to missionary priests. To characterize late Elizabethan Catholicism as (in Christopher Haigh's phrase) "a country-house religion" is an exaggeration, but not much of one. There were established networks of Catholics in London, in Oxford, and other large towns; but they lived precariously, in fear of exposure and double agents[22].

Social Change

In broader terms, the social upheaval bro6ught by the religious changes of Edward's and Elizabeth's reigns was huge. The networks of private charity founded on religious houses, and religious associations (guilds, burial fraternities, chantries, hospitals) were swept away; the damage to education and provision for the poor was enormous. Traditional bonds between neighbours were strengthened by parish ales, between generations by habitual prayer for and remembrance of the dead: all this was abolished. The position of women within society suffered; as well as regularly established convents, there had been numerous religious or quasi-religious associations that had allowed a role and a common life for women both married and unmarried; these too disappeared. All that was left for women were the stark alternatives of marriage or remaining permanently within their parents' household.

James VI and I

As the sixteenth century drew to a close, the problem of the succession to the throne was acute in all minds. Elizabeth was unmarried and childless; there is no firm evidence she ever named a successor. Various candidates were proposed. The strongest, and in the event the successful man, was James VI of Scotland, son to Mary Stuart. Others included Lady Anne Stanley, who descended from Henry VIII's younger sister; Arbella Stuart, James's cousin; and Philip II's daughter, the Infanta Isabella, then Regent of the Netherlands[23]. None of these except James, who had the secret backing of Robert Cecil (son of William), stood a reasonable chance; in the atmosphere of uncertainty, however, interested parties - including English Catholics - made approaches to all of them. When, in March 1603, Elizabeth at last died, Cecil arranged for an Accession Council on the Scottish model to invite James to take the Crown.

There is considerable evidence for James's contact with English Catholics in the years immediately before Elizabeth's death. Amongst the emissaries who met James was Thomas Percy, cousin of the Earl of Northumberland, who certainly believed himself to have received a verbal promise of toleration. James was unsure of the strength of support he was likely to receive in England, and was careful to keep the Catholic population and the large numbers of occasionally conforming "Church Papists" well-disposed. Catholics remained a strong, if declining force, both because of their still considerable numbers and the consideration often given to them by conscientious Catholic rulers. How far James was personally sympathetic to Catholicism, or could feign such sympathy, is unclear; but it would have been consonant with his family history. His mother was devoutly Catholic and died with the circumstances of martyrdom, his son Charles married a Catholic, both his royal grandsons died in the faith - James II lost his throne over it. Moreover there was the recent (1598) example of the Edict of Nantes, by which the French crown extended toleration to its non-Catholic subjects. James's policy as King of Scotland had been ambiguous; some apparent toleration, or at least mitigated persecution, may have been done with an eye to English Catholic opinion. However, English Catholic hopes of toleration might not have been entirely wishful thinking. This would explain the violence of the reaction when these hopes were shown to be illusory.

On arrival south of the Border, James is reputed to have said, "We'll no need the papishes now". His accession had been managed by Robert Cecil, habitually and by breeding anti-Catholic, who was to remain Secretary (and later like his father Lord High Treasurer) until his death in 1612. In 1604, a year after James's accession, Parliament passed an Act for the enforcing of previous statutes against seminary priests, increasing the fines for recusancy, banning Catholics from keeping schools or sending their children abroad for education. In response to a plea for toleration at least of the free exercise of religion in private houses, James issued in September 1604 a proclamation expelling all Catholic priests from the Kingdom. Rather than the wise and tolerant government they had been encouraged to expect, this was persecution worse than any before. For some English Catholics, this was the final, unsupportable act: something must be done.

The Gunpowder Treason

Even today, four hundred years on, every schoolchild knows the story of the Gunpowder Plot. Thirteen Catholic desperadoes conspired to kill the King, and destroy Parliament, by exploding a great store of gunpowder hidden under the House of Commons during the state opening of Parliament on 5th November 1605. A Catholic regime would then have been set up. The plot, however, was exposed when one of the conspirators wrote anonymously to Lord Monteagle, a Catholic peer, warning him to stay away from Parliament. Monteagle took the letter to the King, who at once had Parliament searched; Guy Fawkes, one of the conspirators, was discovered with the powder. He revealed under interrogation the details of the plot, and the remaining conspirators were rounded up at Holbeach House in Staffordshire; some died resisting arrest, the others were taken to the Tower. In this way a dangerous Catholic plot was exposed, and the Crown saved; the consequences for English Catholics were terrible.

There is, unfortunately, no possible way this story, based on the contemporary official account known as "the King's Book", can be true. It is unlikely we shall ever know the true facts of the case; conveniently, the key conspirators died in the assault on Holbeach; or, like Fawkes, were broken under torture and then executed. The official account claims to be based on their testimony. Nevertheless, we can see some immediate problems. First, the gunpowder itself: this was a state monopoly; for a private individual, and (like Fawkes) a Catholic to boot, to be able to acquire thirty-six barrels (enough to destroy the Palace of Westminster in its entirety) from an unspecified source in the midst of London without Government knowledge or connivance is highly improbable. Then the famous Monteagle letter: its

mysterious arrival, and the immediate recognition of its
importance, are suspicious; it gave no detail about the
nature of the plot, and yet the searchers went straight for
the cellar where Fawkes and the powder were hiding. The
cellar itself was leased to Robert Catesby, the
conspiracy's leading light, by an official who
coincidentally died on the morning of November 5th,
1605. Then there are the personnel: all or most of the
conspirators were well-known to Cecil's watchers; Robert
Catesby had been involved in the Earl of Essex's abortive
rebellion in 1601 (as had Francis Tresham, and Lord
Monteagle), and was certainly a marked man. Thomas
Percy, as we have seen, had met King James in Scotland
before Elizabeth's death as a representative of England's
Catholics. Catesby's servant Bates claimed under torture
that Catesby himself had met Cecil late in October 1605.
There is a story that Cecil gave specific instructions that
Percy and Catesby were not to be taken alive. It is strange
that, in the raid on Holbeach, all the conspirators, who
were armed only with swords, were not taken alive by the
two hundred or more sherriff's men with firearms who
surrounded the house. And so it goes on: one suspicious
detail after another. Monteagle, who had made very
public submission to Anglicanism on James's accession,
featured in the confessions made by Fawkes and Thomas
Winter, but all mention of him was removed in the official

copies; he was in 1606 awarded a very substantial Government pension for life. He certainly knew of the plot before the letter reached him (if that story is not a complete fiction); whether he or another was Cecil's principal agent within the conspiracy is unknowable.

A Government Plot?

It seems likely that from first to last, the Plot was fomented by Government agents, as a means of drawing out the more troublesome amongst the Catholic population, and using them to fabricate an excuse to silence permanently calls for tolerance of Catholicism. If so, it succeeded brilliantly, and must rank as one of the longest lasting, and most effective, pieces of government black propaganda in history. Even if we accept the narrative of the King's Book as accurate, we are left with an identical result: an event of European notoriety to the lasting discredit of English Catholics. Perhaps it was truly just a ramshackle conspiracy that had exactly the effect as a finely calculated work by agents provocateurs, of the sort Cecil and Walsingham before him had been executing for decades. The reader must make up his own mind which he thinks more probable.

In the ensuing sweep of the country, numerous priests were arrested, including the scholarly and pious Henry Garnet, superior of the Jesuit mission who had eluded

capture since arriving with Robert Southwell twenty
years beforehand. He, and three other Jesuits, went to the
gallows, although there was demonstrably no connexion
between them and the conspiracy. For reasons of state,
however, Cecil wished to perpetuate the sedulously
encouraged official picture of the relentless conspiracy
between the Pope and his Jesuitical agents, "that blood-
sucking Romish Antichrist with his whole swarm of
shavelings". Within a year, the recusancy laws were
toughened further: Catholics were forbidden to appear at
Court, to live within ten miles of London, or to travel
more than five miles from where they lived without
consent of magistrates; they could not be lawyers or
doctors; the financial penalties for recusancy were further
increased, and more rigorously enforced. Each year, on
November 5th, was set a public celebration of the
deliverance of the state from Catholic conspiracy, so that
the wickedness of the Pope's religion should not be
forgotten. Four hundred years on, the festival on
November 5th is still kept.

Conclusion

The foregoing has I hope given some idea of when and how England stopped being Catholic. As for why: in practical terms, it is because of the seizure of a particular political-economic opportunity by a small but powerful pressure-group of Protestants (by conviction or from expedience), able to manipulate the considerable power of the Tudor state to their ends; which included, either centrally or by implication, the eradication of Catholicism. Why did they do this? Some believed their version of Christianity was true, and that of the Catholics corrupt and wicked, a danger to souls; some that England's strength and independence could be maintained only by a sturdy separation from the continent, and that this political separation required also a religious one; some, particularly in the early years, knew their fortunes were built on the loot of the Church, and that a Catholic restoration might mean disgrace and ruin. For some, all of these notions may have been operative, to a greater or less extent; for others, less reflective, it was simply the policy of the ruling clique, and for this reason to be followed by any who under that regime wished to prosper.

Three quarters of a century after Henry VIII's break with Rome, Catholicism in England was still numerically strong; small but devoted groups of priests brought the sacraments where they could, and in places local magnates and gentry were able to offer some measure of protection from legal penalties. But Catholics were disbarred from Royal service, from the Universities, and all but the lowest reaches of the Law: public life was effectively closed to them. Recusancy fines were enforced sporadically, but could be in the long term crippling. After the Gunpowder Treason, there was no hope of official toleration, nor of a coup domestic or from abroad. Moreover the continual preaching by Protestant divines had some effect in producing a growing body of Englishmen convinced of the value of the state religion; this combined with the persistent propaganda of English Protestant triumph over Papist iniquity (the Armada and the Gunpowder business were, and are, the most durable and effective) to create not just a Protestant state (which was in place by 1559) run by a small number of Protestant magnates, but also a country that was, increasingly, Protestant or at least anti-Catholic by instinct. The slow decline of Catholicism in England had begun, perhaps; but the witness of the martyrs, and the heroism of the ordinary ministry of the hunted priests had provided Catholics with a sense of identity and of the supreme value of the sacramental life that would carry it through even the lean generations to come.

Bibliographical Note

The bibliography of this period is immense; I shall not even attempt a comprehensive book list. A good survey of recent scholarship can be found in Christopher Haigh's *English Reformations* (Oxford, 1993), an excellent and balanced survey. Details of sixteenth century Catholicism and the experience of Catholics can be found in Eamon Duffy's The Stripping of the Altars and The Voices of Morebath, and in J J Scarisbrick's *The Reformation and the English People* (Oxford, 1984); the same author's *Henry VIII* (1968, new edition 1997) remains valuable. From the other side, A G Dickens's 1964 *The English Reformation* is an intelligent reworking of the traditional Whig history, found in magisterial form in such older books as the *Oxford History of England*. All of these works contain extensive additional bibliography.

For more particularly Catholic history, the English Catholic History Association's *Reader's Guide to English Catholic History* is useful. Older works by Catholic writers still contain much of value; Hilaire Belloc wrote prolifically on this period, and can still be read with profit, despite his occasional inaccuracies. Much of his work is out of print, but his *Characters of the Reformation* (1936), and *How the Reformation Happened*

are still available, and worth reading. Hugh Ross
Williamson's *The Gunpowder Plot* (1951) remains
provocative; Philip Caraman's numerous first-rate
historical studies, particularly his excellent *Henry Garnet
and the Gunpowder Plot* are unfortunately for the most
part available only second hand.

Endnotes

1   See, for instance, Owen Chadwick's *The Reformation* (Penguin, 1964), still a
    standard textbook: "The Reformation came because limitation of the power
    of the Church was necessary to the further development of efficient
    government" (p.25)

2   Some scholars suggest that Luther's nailing his theses to the church door is a
    later invention; however this was the standard medieval method of advertising
    a controversial position. If Luther didn't nail them up himself, undoubtedly
    someone else did.

3   Pluralism - one man holding many ecclesiastical positions - was one of the
    constant targets of reformers

4   This had been a favourite conceit of the so-called Conciliarist theologians in
    the preceding century.

5   Her date of birth is disputed; arguments have been made for as early as 1499
    and as late as 1507. Somewhere between the two seems most probable.

6   The Howard family were effectively a cadet branch of the Plantagenets
    (England's royal line before the Tudor usurpation). Anne Boleyn's mother
    was daughter of the second Duke of Norfolk, and sister of the third. At this
    period, we should remember, Dukedoms were quasi-royal titles, given only to
    those of the blood royal or close affinity to it.

7   See Leviticus 18.16 and 20.21

8   This is at best arguable; Henry's affair with Anne's sister had set up exactly
    the same degree of affinity between him and Anne as between him and
    Catherine. If (as Henry claimed) the Pope could not dispense from one, no
    more could he dispense from the other. In fact Henry applied for, and was

granted, a dispensation from this illicit affinity in January 1528, in the hope that his existing marriage would be declared unlawful. He was thus simultaneously admitting and denying the Pope's power to dispense.

9   He could have probably made a stronger case had he not insisted (against her explicit statement) that Catherine's marriage to Arthur had indeed been consummated. A public betrothal, or an unconsummated marriage, established a quite distinct form of impediment to marriage, that of "public honesty", which needed a separate dispensation. Henry VII's agents had not applied for this from Pope Julius, nor had it been granted. Had appeal been made on these technical grounds, there would have been a good chance of its success. There is some evidence that Wolsey wished to do exactly this, but was overruled by the King, who seems to have made the Levitical text his own personal totem in this matter.

10   Cromwell, another lawyer, rose from obscurity in Wolsey's service. From 1533 he holds the office of Secretary of State; from 1536, he is Lord Privy Seal. Another Lutheran sympathizer, he founded a great fortune on the spoils of his office. Oliver Cromwell, rebel against Charles I, Parliamentarian general during the Civil Wars, regicide and "Lord Protector" during the Commonwealth, was his great-nephew.

11   One of the confusions of this period is the changing names of its protagonists. John Dudley becomes first Lord Lisle, then the Earl of Warwick (he claimed, implausibly, descent from the famous Kingmaker), finally Duke of Northumberland. Similarly Edward Seymour is first Viscount Beauchamp, then Earl of Hertford, then Duke of Somerset. These changes of name can obscure the close connexions between the principal players in the Protestant camp. Seymour's daughter Anne married Dudley's son John.

12   Suggestions that he suffered from syphilis are probably unfounded; his chronically ulcerated legs are more likely to be evidence of osteomyelitis from unhealed thigh fractures than tertiary syphilis, which his doctors would have been well able to recognize and (after their fashion) treat.

13   The widely held opinion that any orders conferred using this Ordinal could not be considered those of a Catholic priest was confirmed in 1896 by Pope Leo XIII's encyclical *Apostolicae Curae*, which judged Anglican orders to be invalid, not least because of defects in this text.

14   In 1571, he was made Baron Burghley. His younger son, Robert, in turn became Secretary of State in 1590, after the death of Walsingham. Robert Cecil was made Earl of Salisbury in 1605; the family still holds the title.

15 This refusal, or recusancy, becomes the defining mark of Catholics from this time; they are often known simply as recusants (Latin *recusare*, "to refuse").

16 It took some time before enough clergymen with any pretension to episcopal orders (none had been Bishops under Mary) could be collected to consecrate Parker; at the time this was done, the Edwardine Ordinal, which was the rite used, had not been reinstated by Parliament, so even by the loose standards of Elizabethan churchmanship we may honestly doubt both the validity and liceity of this action. The claim made in 1604 by Christopher Holywood SJ that the ceremony took place in the Nag's Head in Fleet Street is probably merely scurrilous; in its bearing on the (obvious and permanent) breach in the Apostolic Succession of Anglican orders at this juncture, it is entirely superfluous.

17 Famously, John Henry Newman's Anglican *Tract* 90 of 1841 attempted to do this. It can best be seen as an exercise in ingenuity. The plain text of the Articles is designedly anti-Catholic.

18 It was nailed to the door of the Bishop of London's palace by John Felton, a recusant gentleman, who was subsequently executed. His son, Thomas, was moved by this to go into exile, become a Franciscan, and was himself put to death in 1588. The father was beatified in 1886, the son in 1929.

19 Such are the Ridolfi Plot, the Squire Plot, and numerous smaller affairs - all are fairly implausible, probably built on a trace amount of genuine intent against the State, and were presented as propaganda coups for Protestantism. Typically, Jesuits feature as the arch-villains of the piece.

20 In 1569, Cecil (against the explicit instructions of the Queen) had seized the bullion being shipped to pay Spanish troops in the Low Countries, whilst at harbour in England under safe-conduct. This meant the imposition of an otherwise unnecessary, and highly unpopular, local tax to make good the loss.

21 Haigh, *English Reformations*, p.21

22 The career of the playwright Christopher Marlowe is a fascinating case in point. He for a while passed as a Catholic in England and in the Low Countries, but (it appears) was all the time a paid agent of Secretary Walsingham. His violent death in 1593 was very likely the result of some secret service intrigue.

23 She would have been, from a Catholic point of view, the ideal candidate; but the Spanish Crown had neither the will, nor the money, to promote her candidacy.